WALKING AGAINST THE SPIRITS OF UNMARRIED LIFE

OGHENEOVO BENJAMIN OLORI

Table of Contents

INTRODUCTION

This subject could sound strange to Non – Africans because of the unfamiliar and manner in which some of the terms are perceived and how marriage is seen in Africa. Majority of Westerners do not hold anything against the gods or appease the ancestral powers neither holds the rights of others to themselves because of their understanding of their own environment. Additionally, marriages in Africa have their own spirits - peculiarity from the Western and Asian world. The underlying emphasis on how family decisions affect many who wish to get married has become a matter of concern. Generally, marriage is hinged on both traditional – cultural – philosophical – psychological – couselling or sociological angles.

For whatever reason, many families do not want their children to get married or marry their choice of man or woman as a result of THE SPIRITS OF UMARRIED RULING IN THEIR FAMILY LIVES. This could occur due to unnecessary intention, hatred, jealousy, pride, family wickedness, ancestral revocation, inheritance and witchcraft exhibition to hunt and to deprive those who wished to get married. While some insist on getting married to wealthy men or ladies with exemption of few who lives for God, these factors are majorly controlled by poor parental background, poor manners, strong appetite for sex or unsatisfied sexual urge, lack of sextual urge, unclassified individual personality and get rich quick syndrome or selfish desire etcetera etcetera.

Those who experience or posses these characteristics hardly know or easily ignored them due to the benefits inherent in them, they act as carterlist. Once you know or identify any of these, TAKE A DRASTIC STEP, WALK OUT OF IT AND GET YOUR FREEDOM.

Sometimes, if you decide to walk against the wishes of those who do not want you to get married to the person of your choice, the decision - makers in your family might go extra miles against you in diabolic form to ensure there is no fruit of the womb, constant miscarriages of pregnancy, financial hardship, indebtedness, ill – health, invocation of criminal case, unforeseen happenings, unhappy family life and invocation of infidelity spirit that could eventually terminates the marriage to achieve their aims. In most cases, individuals behaviour – pride and impatience could be hindrance too. Although, many westerners do not believe in these characteristics as factors working against peoples progress but Africans do.

WALK OUT WITHOUT ACCEPTING THEIR PRESSURE!! DO NOT PLEASE ANYONE NEITHER ALLOW ANYBODY TO MAKE YOUR DECISION. BEAR THE BAD AND ENJOY THE GOOD.

People are often reluctant to commit to a walkout because they think it brings too much pain, either physical pain or spiritual one. But if you just give it a try, you 'll make two pleasant discoveries.

You 'll love walking out this way because it produces pleasure and no pain. You 'll experience a level of physical vitality you 've never felt before - Robbins, 1991; p447;2.

The book was written to showcase life experience usually encounter by men and women with emphasis to an African family as a case study. Some parents and relatives think that, by asking their children not to marry a particular person could be a way of protecting them from harm or giving them security based on what they most have heard about the man or woman or their families. This warning could be due to the fact; if the man or woman is very poor or someone with questionable character.

However, some parents do not want their wealth to be transferred to poor families and as such, they always stand against their children marrying from poor homes in order to retain and increase their influence in society because in Africa, rich families do not identify much with the poor, especially on marital affairs. This behavioral pattern has deprived many from getting married at when due or not getting married at all. And those who wish to go against his or her family decision could face antagonism. This does not mean that; individual wishing to get married without family approval is always successful in their marriage (that is, it not a guarantee to be successful in marriage being that one takes a personal decision) if such relationship is built on fatuation, love of money and individuals personality rather than real love.

While some go into marriage just to have children and quite thereafter. They group do nott want to be answerable to any man or any woman after they must have achieved their feets or when they considered their partner not to be **the ideal person.** Bartering, nagging and transfer of anger are other factors that could de – generate into crises in relationship - marriage.

It is also displayed in marital statistics that many relationships – marriages often fails if the man or the woman knows that; there is no family support. Most especially when problems occur, there is nobody to complaint to or to be called upon to address the issue. This raises the fear of unforeseen occurrence makes many to outline all issues with both families and to give respect to both sides.

Somehow, some families would insist that their well trained son or daughter should not marry uneducated person or someone without good characters.

Of course, many marriages or arranged marriages by parents of the same standard (wealthy parents) usually fails. Infact, some do not last up to a year after marriage because the marriage was built on extrinsic and not intrinsic motivation (material things and not love).

An individual making a decision of his or her own life must design a templates of logical reasoning, must be independent of self and be able to analyze situations in the environment. Such a person should be able to interpret utterances and behavioural patterns from people either in his or her favour or against him or her. This is not to say, peoples views should be your compass. Those who pretend or voice actions should be on the template to deduce those that loves or hate him when in relationship.

Chapter 1

RESIST FAMILY FORCES

Rick Seba and Tilda Fox identified a lot of factors in their relationship and walked against them. They walked against the spirits of unmarried *lives intentionally arranged by Tilda Fox's mother and family.*

While this book was underdevelopment, my nephew Ochuko who was dating Sophia read through the manuscript and aired his views on the manners African parents treats their children as it regards to marital affairs and said, *''I can equally walk against my parents, when I sense there are people within me trying to deprive me of my choice of lady to marry. I can't allow someone to deprive me of my happiness.''*

Walking against them could be good in a moment and only if you will not fall back to your parents on anything especially when problems occur in your marital life.

Does walking against them means everlasting isolation of self from your parents for denying you of your happiness?

Yemi replied the question during a random sampling survey, *''it all depends on how they took the situation. It doesn't mean disrespect but respecting my right and independency is a key to peace''.*

In his late forties, Rick Seba terminated a lot of relationships - lovers – real love on the bases of divine providence until Tilda Fox was introduced to him as a single, beautiful and intelligent nurse who had a few heart – breaks for the sake of her mother's wishes.

Spinning the wheel of love to catch up with the newly unseen lady, Rick Seba empirically called on her +2348036341907 mobile phone to ensure an entrant into the heart of Tilda Fox. To justify her mother's tyrant act, Tilda declined and resisted strongly the marriage proposal on phone due to un-acquaintances of Rick Seba's conceptualized image by her mother. Coupled with the fear of her mother who always wished her daughters to marry only staunch rich men.

Tilda Fox quickly realized this unnecessary marriage denial as a factor and also consider that age is not in her favour. *''Marrying only a rich man''* a word that is usually used by Mrs. Night Fox, is a family force truncating Tilda's progress through the hard decisions of her mother against her life. After weighing the '*'ought''* as a philosophical tools, Tilda prayed fervently and cancelled her mother's decision on who to marry.

Many a times, African society sees the cancellation of this kind of decision against one's life as an act of disobediencc to God and to parents, if a child rejects the decisions of the elderly. This brought to mind a checklist; a choice, a decision and an issue of human right which is under estimated and misinterpreted in most cases. The questions are, should parents and family members takes decision for an adult who wishes to marry? At what age should adult be tele – guided on who he or she should marry? Should the rights of the person who chooses to marry be considered by parents and family members? Does the marriage serves the advantage or disadvantages of the family member or the person who chooses to marry?

Rick Seba meeting with Tilda for the very first time after their phone conversation sponge out diametric reasons why providence designed both of them for each other. In their first engagement, Tilda Fox spelt out some phenomenal in a man by pulling down a man who posses anger, pride and boastfulness. Thus, *''my man should not be stupendously rich for now, a God loving friend, hardworking, intelligent with calligraphic writing, peaceful, a man who will be thoughtful of her and respect her person, no battering, a patience man, trustworthy, a man who can persevere and easy going, a man who will allow me to continue attending my KGS church''.*

As soon as Mrs. Night Fox perceived the engagement in line with the cordial relationship between her daughter and Rick Seba, she turned to aggressive ghost, determined to terminate their lives if they insist on getting married without her consent as a mother. She displayed her nomenclature tag to her *'' I will enter the sea and hidden valley's to destroy Rick Seba for taking to himself mine daughter! The best of my daughters without my approval!. I shall deal heavily with him!!!''.*

To be candid, many have lost their lives, kidnapped, maimed and humiliated as a result of insisting on marrying a man or a woman of their choice against the decisions of their parents or family members. This calls for enmity when disagreement occur between parents and their son or daughter. Like the American adage; *''when injustice becomes law, resistance becomes a duty''.* The act of depriving an adults from marrying who they chooses is an act of injustice which has being rated as normal in Africa culture.

How does this African belief in tandem with contemporary society or globalization where autonomy, non – maleficence, beneficence and justice holds ways?

Bolatito and Lanre gave answers to the question through comparative instances in ethics: *autonomy*;- it refers to the *capacity* of the human *person* to choose freely as a *rational being* who possesses the *cognitive* power to *informed choices*. This capacity in human being is the foundation in which human dignity and respect is built. It is upon this principle that Rick and Tilda took their decision to move on in spite of the turbulent and worrisome decision from Tilda's family .

The issue of depriving adults of getting married should not be lumped on the third party decision as *non-maleficence* does not give room to harm anyone physically or psychologically base on his or her choice or freedom it relates. As *justice and fairness are requires to ease the burdens of authorities working against unmarried and married lives.*

The life of Rick Seba is like the proverbial night cat who had sails in the ocean without a ship, wet, dredged under the rain and stunning thunders, without food in a rocky burning bush without water. He shows highest respect to everyone but fears no death. He considered incessant threat to his life by his mother – in-law to be, as a threat to herself and sue her to the traditional council to retract her verbose and contaminated statements for peace and justice accord or face collateral damage.

Mrs. Night Fox resisted all attempt for peaceful resolution against all odds like Putin of Russia against Ukrainians. She scuttled all moves at the family level and keyed into diabolic means to achieve her goals like the biblical Prophets of Baal.

Rick Seba rich in ideas, dare Mrs. Night Fox to tie – the – nut with Tilda Fox in spite of the looming danger posed by her mother – immediate family to lose her position as the first daughter as well as to forfeit her inheritance from her late fathers Will.

Reliance on her tested trust and love for Rick Seba whom she perceives as desired for future wealthy man and for the sake of his complex gentleness without mixed reaction made Tilda to swim in undiluted love. An independent Tilda continuously kicks at the militarization character of her mother and dare the entire family for consequences of her decision to marry Rick Seba being considered as a poor and unbred aged man. Is Rick Seba really an old man as postulated by my mother? Tilda Fox inquired intrinsically with a conclusion for an answer that; *''mine Rick Seba is only undergoing hardship hence his appearance seems like that of an old man. But……. I am equally seeing an illuminating handsome bright scholar who desires wealth through strong ideas of the pen to rule the world''.*

Tilda never loses grip or hope for the accorded poor man. Both shared intelligent ideas with little polarization on religion belief system based on their foundations. Rick Seba later pollinates her fiance with biblical rhetorics and meanings from the original scroll of the universal law to draw demarcation on various christian beliefs as it relates to Hebrews and Greeks mythology.

In order to purge her mother stronghold against her desire, Tilda decided to verge into womanhood to mystify the decision of her family against her future plans by getting pregnant with the intention to soften the minds of her mother, to move from unmarried life and barenesss. Rather, the news of the pregnancy wrecked more tones of harder ex – communication influenced by her mother, elder brother and her immediate younger sister. Tilda believes, stand and justification for her dying in love could not be exhumed by anyone.

With tilk – talk they say; *''she has been hypnotized by Rick Seba hence Tilda's decision is irrational''* but it isn't true, its just to give a bad name to a dog in order to justify their hatred in hanging it.

Rick Seba finally tied – the – nut with Tilda at the Customary Registry with the signature of her father's younger sister, Crates Nitive and other well-wishers who energized the couple's day merrily, merrily, merrily, merily life is but a honey.

Rick Seba dramatized a hearty song of love in rendition to his newly married wife who is no longer Tilda Fox by virtue of legal status of the marriage at the Customary Registry but now known and should be called Mrs. Tilda Rick. The voice during the rendition appears solo and later followed by soprano and bass without jazz, opening wonders of imagination by invited guest and visitors anchoring along one voice in many. Sing, sing, sing…..

Lordly - lovely over the Queen, she made me a genius via soft counseling to achieve goals and

aspirations while she de – energizes wrong thought of me. A Queen!! Indeed…… A Queen she is. A lover Queen, Mine Queen, My Queen through which establishment of more great ideas emanated. A Queen that replicated a handsome lion of the tribe of Judah to which all honour kiddles love in building peace and greatness.

In order to be successful in her relationship that metamorphosed into marriage, Mrs. Tilda surround herself with those who affirms that everything she does was right. She avoid those who denied her from marital enjoyment and she was convinced about the decision against the unmarried umpires while she devalue them publicly, applauded herself openly and correct the wrong of her opposers.

The pregnancy became due and she delivered a baby boy at the Federal Medical Center. On the hospital bed, she put a call across to her mother, Mrs. Night Fox, informing her of the safe delivery and blessing of the Lord upon which a new child has being added to the family.

In response to Mrs. Tilda on phone, Mrs. Night Fox quarried in severity; *does it mean you were pregnant before now? How come where you able to deliver the baby alive? Ah!!! Oh! No! You mean you have being put to bed?* She lamented the unusual and unexpection that beats her imaginations; that worked against her demonic conjure – Africa black powers - witchcraft – spiritual missiles to be carried out to terminate Tilda during child birth in order to hold her husband responsible on the ground that he killed their daughter. Known to be a terrifying being who usually played the role of the Philistine giant or Goliath of Gath, dread many to approach her for a discussion over her cause to intimidate and humiliate anyone on the acceptance of Tilda as a daughter again.

The God that never sleeps nor slumber, the Lion of the tribe of Judah, the Only One God Jehovah showed compassion to those he loves. *''He (God) carried us through the evil judges and acquitted us. Even when we pass the shadow of death, we fear no evil''*. Reciting the power in the Psalmist moved the newly married couple to scale through the snare of death set before them as a result of their personal decision to get married against the spirits of unmarried life propounded by Mrs. Night Fox - family.

Africa is unlike Europe and Asia. Unmarried person is seen as a social misfit, irresponsible, and demonic or witchcraft who must have gotten married or have children in the spirit world or coven. At old age, he or she (is prescribed as a witch) is scorned at and maltreated. This is one major reason why everyone wishes to marry and raise children in Africa. Suffix it to say, there are some communities in Nigeria like the eastern states that have a lot of unmarried ladies due to culture that specified certain obligations which the suitor most meet financially. That is to say, the inability of the man to meet the high demands of the lady's family could lead to marriage denial or end up without marriage.

And again, there are families that are seen as caused because, there is no single lady that is seen to be legally married in the entire family or community but they indulge in marital sex with various men, raise children and care for them without getting married which has become a standard in their families. While some are termed slaves. This yoke must be broken. It must be broken via your personal decision, by honest prayers to God and fasting and nothing else but walk into your victory.

Chapter 2

Living in Reality

Little wonders that pains and more wonder of stress couple with critical care nursing job, house core, education of self, financial handicap and rearing of newly born baby became a challenge. Mrs. Tilda Rick is naturally gifted with power beyond what is normal to withstand castigation of all sort and her endurance is a patch for many young ladies to emulate including her wiliness to accomplish a goal and promises made before Rick Seba.

A lot of people cannot differentiate reality from fantasy in a relationship but this new couple did.

At a point, to be precise, 27 May, 2020 Rick Seba and Tilda started life and living. They cured the darkness, emptiness and vanity that crept into their human system from their independent decisions that erupted chaos from envious old mother. Sorry and sorrow of parental abandonment before, during after their marital vows left the entire burden of love and happiness pierced through their ears so far.

Mama, Crates Nitive who was in the pictures of their hard times, encourages the newly married couple with twinkle - multi experiences in order to overcome a depressing thoughts caused by Mrs. Night Fox, had paid off. Grand Ma as she's fondly called, bridged the vacuum of motherhood interior that was created by Mrs. Night Fox. Mama settles dispute of various degrees and energizes the newly married couple's to face the world of reality in spite of the plague of envy and unnecessary hatred by Tilda's family.

To care for the new born baby, Mrs. Create Nitive traveled a hundreds kilometers to visit the couple in Delta Headquarters' where she spent a considerable one month with them before living for Warfi. She made calls from time to time in order to direct how to care for the child and what to apply when needed.

One would have expected that; with all the troubles, denials and with birth of new baby, the family Goliath will relent the blowing of her evil arrows.

Living in reality gave rise to more unforeseen occurrence as Pastor Kutis Fox, the elder brother of Tilda, used his domineering position without fair - hearing to force Tilda from KGS Church by importing sentimental headache of his immediate family to hunt after the battled young lady (Tilda) by quoting unfamiliar biblical laws that says; ''if marriage approval is not given by family custodians, such a person should be disfellowship'' a means to achieve their bid against Tilda's marriage. Mrs. Night Fox worked hard with Pastor Kutis Fox to ensure the refusal of Tilda bride prize to enable the church to hold onto this as their principle to ex – communicate the young lady with flimsy excuses. Pastor Kutis Fox is a man known to be swinging in the direction of his mother's without good personal attitude to sue for peace nor forgiveness in his spirit just like his mother.

Series of church meetings attended by Tilda's friends unveil the strategies adopted to leach psychological trauma on Tilda as well as to embarrass her publicly for not hidden to her mother's decision to marry a staunch rich man. Those who supported Tilda's personal decision to continue with her life where scorned and perceived as enemies within.

One of the church elders, Brother Simsim Jakum was heard saying; ''we are amazed with the influence of Tilda's mother in the family and Pastor Kutis Fox unchristian behaviour towards his immediate younger sister. It shows he lacks administrative acumen to handle issues of serious concern. And I think, when a similar issues like this occurs in church in the future, references will be made to the roles he played previously which could reduce his pedigree to speak on other peoples affairs. Infact, I'm highly disappointed in him as a Minister''.

To buttress various comments by Tilda's supporters on the ill – treatment by her immediate family, Dr. Mrs. Peroko Olfa aggressively emphases that; ''how would they force a lady above forties not to marry whoever she chooses to marry in the guess to satisfy her mother's personal needs and wishes. This is wickedness and arrant devilish act that should not be heard of christians.''

Many counsellor's could tell you that; it is better to stay single than going into marriage that is full of trouble''. Citting examples of men who killed their wives in marriage. Yes, the truth is, there is no marriage on earth that is free of encumbrances. Those involves are managing each other. The sweet names they calls themselves in public and the humility you see them displays in public are not 50/50 nor 100%. If you can recall how God lamented in creating mankind, it could give us a clue that our marriages are at the Mercies of God. It is only people with inpatient, pride, arrogant selfish desires without love for God and their partners that easily brakes – up their marriages.

When you see married partners fighting, abusing themselves, it is the spirit that never wanted them to marry that is raising its ugly heads. This is not to say; there is no peaceful marriages where high level of submission, respect and pure love for each other is not in existence.

In all, Tilda never gives up in doing God's work which later led to her reinstatement after a period of eight months of ex – communication from the church. Her reinstatement was a declaration of wisdom from those who fought behind doors against her family wider plough across the administrative leadership of KGS.

Just as God can't lie, the narration of the hidden agenda of the unfaithfuls is loaded with lies - they lie here and there to high heaven to circumvent the truth. They mopped out a mountainous lies to whoever that cares to listen in order to fortify their earlier stand to scuttle Tilda image with unjustifiable gain.

In the scope of their bibles, there seems to be no forgiveness or probably they do not believe in it but they preach it as sermon wherever they go while working contrary to the christian faith they claims to profess. They holds strongly to the reason while Mrs. Tilda disobeyed their decisions and to worsen it she got pregnant with a startling picture of sinner on her. Perhaps, they do not know that ''the redemption'' is not for the angels already dwelling with God in heavens.

Theologians should be able to give the statistics of those whom have sinned from the human population as recorded in the holy scriptures in Romans 3:9 – 23, to justify who can be judge. The scriptures is explicit on every matter in line with this, an African adage says; those who lives in a glass house should not throw stones at others to avoid retaliation that could pull breakable glasses on their heads.

It was obvious that Mr. Rick Seba went to Tilda's family to ask her hands in marriage and Tilda spoke to them on a passionate ground on the reasons she considered Mr. Rick Seba to be her husband. However, all efforts proved abortive on the alleged bases that; Mr. Rick Seba has no job, no shelter to lay his head, he has no money, he has many wives and many children from concubines with all manners of lies to dissuade Tilda from marriage. It was at this point the two lovers went for Customary Registry to continue their lives irrespective of the provocation, denial and threat to life from Tilda's family.

The United Nations and African Union Charter on Human Rights and Privileges are Universal Declaration that safe guard every human in issue of decision making as it relates to this subject. Thus; ''

Chapter 3

Dwelling with the Spirit of Unforgiveness

Their provocation implies that *''weak people revenge.''*

If you're not being treated with love and respect, check your ''price tag''. Perhaps you have marked yourself down. It's you who tell people what you're worth by what you accept. Get off the clearance rack and get behind the glass where they keep all the valuables. ''That's where you belong''.

Mrs. Tilda occupied the glass and her refusal to be at the rack provoked Mrs. Isbama Twak as their failing plans were observed all over her appearances without a left out in speeches.

Me!!! ''I will never have anything to do with the corrupt Tilda nor my children with her children'' said Mrs. Isbama Twak who is the immediate younger sister to Mrs. Tilda.

Mrs. Isbama Twak abandons her marriage and took her children in the custody of her mother as - the – mother wishes.

Tilda holds on to her husband unlike Mrs. Isbama Twak who deserted her marriage on the ground of proofing financial superiority above her husband, on the bases of her mother questioning the financial nitty – gritty of the man, has taken up hatred feathers against Mrs. Tilda. *''Tilda chooses to marry a poor old man. A man who has no house of it own. Yet, she's talking about what the future holds for the man. Who does that in this twenty first century?''* quarried Mrs. Isbama Twak. *''Since Tilda chooses to marry a man who is not anointed by our mother, that marriage is non and void and troubles continues till God's kingdom come.''* She took to herself the position of the Pharisees whose judgment was instantaneous and was eager to cast stones and very ready, leading the campaign of blackmailing her elder sister in all front to score their goals against Tilda's right.

This brings to mind the unforgiving spirits posses by them. In spite of all the teaching of Christ at KGS and the counseling from the temple of elders, it shows neither assimilation nor change of heart. It is upon this similar scenario that, Apostle Peter was caught saying; *''for the time has come for judgment to begin at the house of God and if it begins within us first, what will be the end of those who do not obey the gospel of God*? It postulated the danger that will befalls the evil ones that lives in the church but hidden their hearts.

Joining hands in the unholy fight against Tilda's marriage is Barrister Tugbumu Fox who helps their mother to confiscate and change their fathers Will in favour of Mrs. Night Fox in exclusion of Tilda and her twin brother Mr. Chap Fox. Mr. Chap Fox stood against their mother – family decision and insisted that his twin sister must be left alone to make her own choice on the matrimonial issue. Barrister Tugbumu Fox also instituted a legal matter against Mrs. Isbama Twak's husband on the bases of not being the owner of the house they built together while in marriage. An initiative by Mrs. Night Fox to terminate that marriage as well because the man also appears to be a poor man and uncontrollable before them.

Narrating the subjugation of Mrs. Night Fox who has ordained herself as a god in the family where men stand talless and without ideas of their own to rule over her enthusiasm to truncate progress.

''Come to think of it, Chief Dr. Fox divorced Mrs. Night Fox before he died as if he was a prophet that foresaw the event in the future. Yet she parades herself as Mrs. Fox in the family corridor of decision makers and twisted the hands of the clock. Has she forgotten how she was accused of being the killer of her husband by the same people she frantalise with? It is an indication that she did it to inherit what belong to the children with the way she's going........'' said, Watt Motr.

A lot of boosting and gossip have taken the stage in spiritual and physical with high tension every where. At this time, nobody cares neither ready to soften pedder. Arranged ranger of influence is being showcased on daily bases as it's being reported by mediators and crises fuellers. Mr. Rick Seba and his wife has taken the stage not to succumb towards inferior arguments without the application of logical reasoning. Both sees Mrs. Night Fox and those co – jointed, fighting the unjust course as infinitesimal beings who are not properly integrated into the society from birth.

Mr. Rick Seba was heard saying to a member of KGS who acted as a intermediary; '' children can only be forced while adults can only be compared with the trigger of a gun. Even at this, we can never be deterred by their actions. In several cases, crises in the world over is caused by forcing people to go against their wishes or due to denial of ones right or intruding into ones territories. Traditions has toppled individuals right as singing, tradition demands!!!. Does it mean if your tradition demands that you should kill and sacrify humans you will do just so? Does tradition surpassed natural - law – of justice? Does thoughts stronger than logic? If tradition matter most why do they embrace christianity or are they neither here or there''?

The KGS church could not extinguished the erupted crises. Perhaps, the temple of elders was afraid to rule against the stand of Pastor Kutis Fox on the matter due to his personal influence on the Church Board. To please him, they laid emphasis on Tilda wrong doing and the place of tradition which she failed to recognize.

Of course, KGS church handles the matter with naivety and referred them back to the family where Tilda's mother hold sway, swig in Eldorado and as the final arbita in the midst of the oldest men who dread her powers, easily conceded and where justice cannot be obtained is now the court of jurisdiction.

Weak people revenge, strong people forgive, intelligent people ignore. Tired, but I will keep up the fight. I have the hope both sure and firm, be nice to people because the world can be very difficult and all need a little help sometimes. Rather than taking matters into our own hands, let us be determined to be loyal and wait patiently on Jehovah to correct matters while waiting upon the Almighty God who only can defend the weak in their state of ignoramus.

Being ignorance of the universal laws, even when Mrs. Night Fox is fully aware that her daughter is legally married with a baby in her foetus, she went ahead to arranged for another man to marry Tilda on the bases that the man lives in London. This is Africa. Africa where everyone believes that whoever that lives in America, Calada, United Kingdom, Australia, Qatar and not Cameroon, Ghana, Kenya, Gabon, Liberia and Nigeria, are considers to be wealthy in nature.

Tilda's mother never knew this man but on the bases of connection and re-connection from one of her aunty who arranged this Londonia on the ground of what they could benefit and with the mind to thwart Rick Seba's happiness. The reason of re-arranging their married daughter for another man beats the imagination of many people. They thought by giving Tilda's phone number to the Londonian to call her could change everything.

Eventually, the man called severally without positive response. Tilda quarried the link up by her mother. They didn't know this man neither what he is doing for a living in London. What a hell with them? Tilda's response again infuriated her mother - family and crises ensue.

All lovers of peace came into the matter to ensure peaceful part between them. But whenever, the word ''just leave Tilda alone to live her life'' is mentioned, flames appears and if the peace – maker does not go there with fire extinguishers, he or she could get burnt with a standby fueller, Mrs. Twak who lied against her husband for assassination.

Rick Seba's family visited Tilda's mother to discuss a peace part for peaceful resolution. Mrs. Night Fox refused to open door for them. They stood outside appealing and apologizing for the root of no wrong. Their appeal fell on deaf ears as Mrs. Twak was speaking erroneously as a back – up to kindle the fire.

At another occasion, the church committee that dreadfully avoided the matter from it dressing room, only forced itself from the shell of fear after the transfer of Pastor Kutis Fox from the branch where Mr and Mrs Rick's receives weekly Holy Communion. An invitation was sent to the couple's to attend to questioning and to answer questions on how to draft another strategies for solution. In all, the questioning where fired against Tilda to accept the position of being wrong in order to soften the appeal before her mother for easy acceptance with an African belief that says; ''mother cannot wrong a child''. This position was heavily contested in that meeting, unvailing injustice, bias, and ill covering against Tilda's right.

The set up of the last meeting was led to the delegation of committee members to visit Tilda's mother for more appeal to accept her daughter but Mrs Night Fox also ridiculed them. Even at that, the church committee pressurized Tilda to stake her life and continue appealing to the god of her mother. Probably, the gods of her mother that never hears nor sees will listen to her appeal.

This decision was vehemently met with opposition from the newly married couple and Mr Rick Seba quarried the integrity of the committee on the ground of their refusal to appeal to the mother and Pastor Kutis Fox to die the matter in their hearts rather than putting pressure only on the young couple to do the unsual.

In the words of Mr Rick Saba to the committee, ''you guys alway push us to appeal to the mother who have no forgiveness in her heart. While can't you talk her over to let go the matter? Is that you people considered us to be too small or people you can talk to? Oh! Now I know! You don't want to offend Mrs Night Fox due to fear but you deem it fit to be addressing us as if we wrong her. What wrong have we committed that cannot be forgiven? Enough of these. You guys could not talk on the matter when Pastor Kutis was in this branch for fear of disorganizing the committee. It is now you can talk.''

The committee chairman perceived Rick response as a slap and ruled that the committee should withdraw from the matter which they honourably did.

Inview of the immediate circumstances, you should give thanks to the father. Worship and praise Him, no matter what! ''In everything give thanks: for this is the will of God in Christ Jesus concerning you'' (1

Thessaloniana 5:18). Constant prayers helps to walk against this spirit.

Chapter 4

Hope in Advance

Being a nurse, Tilda must have read through the historical anteccedent of Florence Nightingale who was persuaded by her parents to do their biddings but she refused and decided to follow the voice of reason – social humanity. Her mother penned, *''we are two ducks, my husband and I, have given birth to a wild swan''*. In the biography of Florence Nightgale, her mother was written to be so wrong, for Florence was not a wild swan but eagle due to her role in Crimean War.

Rather than taking care, Tilda takes a chance, she takes charge and control. She refuted all kinds of negative fates that her family impose on her like Florence of 1851. In her words; *''I had a lot of opposition immediately I decided to make my own choice of man. My opposition was not from the congregation but from those of the same foetus with me, However, KGS congregation has been so supportive in their love and prayers.''*

None of us can point to what could happen to our lives any moment from now and as such, calling for the life and death of our enemies is not an achievement but a harmful effects of weakness and idiotic life style of people without salvation.

There are historical witnesses such as; Ministers Emmanuel Emmao and Nyaeke whom were spiritually built to extend their souls to satisfy the afflicted souls. They promises were like of the convenant between Christ and his sheeps.

****At her early forties, Tilda was engendered with suitors who are not the likelihood of her mother's choice. Almost crossing the redline of getting a suitor was when Rick Sebas got linked to her. The riddles of denial by Mrs. Tilda Rick's mother -family was a testimonial that the task is huge ahead to face the scoping in reality because they wanted* *her to continue working for them while they siphon her monthly salaries to care for themselves.*

BIBLOGRAPHY

1.Robbins A. (1991) Awaken the Giant Within, Free Press, A Division of Simon & Schuster, Inc. New York.

2.New World Translation of the Holy Scriptures (2013) Published by Watchtower Bible & Track Society of Pennsylvania, U.S.A.

3. Ibid.

4. Roy E. Gane (2021)Adult Sabbath School, Bible Study Guide, 2nd Quarter Achaksprints Jebfindax Limited.

5. Ibid. pg. 144

6. Joyce Meyer (2006) The Confident Woman, Faith Words Hachette Book Group, U.S.A.

7. Bolatito & Lanre(2014) Ethics and Public Affairs, University of Ibadan Press, Ngeria.

www.ingramcontent.com/pod-product-compliance
Lightning Source LLC
LaVergne TN
LVHW020525160826
845677LV00015B/3897

ABOUT THE BOOK

African parents can go extral mile in making decisions for their adult children inspite of the fact that these adults have their lives to live. This book is a life experience of an African family.

Ogheneovo Benjamin Olori is a writer who always tailores his works on experience or based on emperical.

ISBN 9798371470027
90000
9 798371 470027

LEADERSHIP:

POWER, PROCESS AND MANAGEMENT

GETTING YOURSELF FIT FOR THE NEXT TASK

John S. Coughlin